Alice in Credit Land

By Lucy Fedra and Ben Cahalan

With Illustration Selection and Editing by
Annamaria Guadalupe Ochoa

**An Official
Vice Presidents Anonymous
Publication**

Visit our website at **www.StillwaterPress.com** for more information.

First Stillwater River Publications Edition

Library of Congress Control Number: 2018943237

ISBN-13: 978-1-946-30057-7
ISBN-10: 1-946-30057-8

1 2 3 4 5 6 7 8 9 10

Written by Lucy Fedra and Ben Cahalan
Illustrations Selected and Edited by Annamaria Guadalupe Ochoa
Published by Stillwater River Publications, Pawtucket, RI, USA.

Publisher's Cataloging-In-Publication Data
(Prepared by The Donohue Group, Inc.)

Names: Fedra, Lucy. | Cahalan, Ben. | Ochoa, Annamaria Guadalupe, illustrator, editor.
Title: Alice in Credit Land / by Lucy Fedra and Ben Cahalan; with illustration selection and
     editing by Annamaria Guadalupe Ochoa.
Description: First Stillwater River Publications edition. | Pawtucket, RI, USA : Stillwater River
     Publications, [2018] | "An Official Vice Presidents Anonymous Publication."
Identifiers: ISBN 9781946300577 | ISBN 1946300578
Subjects: LCSH: Financial services industry--United States--Humor. | Banks and banking--
     United States--Humor. | Loans--United States--Humor. | Credit--United States--Humor. |
     Carroll, Lewis, 1832-1898. Alice's adventures in Wonderland--Adaptations. | Satire,
     American. | LCGFT: Humor.
Classification: LCC PN6231.F47 F44 2018 | DDC 818.602--dc23

*The views and opinions expressed in this book are solely those of the authors
and do not necessarily reflect the views and opinions of the publisher.*

Alice in Credit Land

Once upon a time, there was a girl named Alice, who saved all of her pennies to buy a house.

She put all of her pennies in a piggy bank.

One day she found the house of her dreams.

The house came with a real estate agent.

The real estate agent came with a mortgage broker.

Alice didn't have enough pennies to the buy the whole house.

"No problem!" said the mortgage broker. "You give us 50 pennies right now from your piggy bank, and we'll find the 10,000 pennies you need to buy the whole house."

"You're so wonderful!" said Alice.

"All you have to do is give us 100 pennies a month for the next 30 years," said the mortgage broker.

"But I only make 40 pennies a month."

"THAT'S ALL?!" screeched the real estate agent as he fell down in shock.

"No problem," soothed the mortgage broker. "Just give us 20 pennies a month."

"You're so wonderful!!" said Alice.

"Just for the first year," said the mortgage broker.

"What happens after that?" asked Alice.

"The payments go up," said the mortgage broker.

"How much?" asked Alice.

Don't know," said the mortgage broker.

"What if I don't have enough pennies when the payments
go up?"

"But you will!!!" screamed the broker. *"You'll get a
raise. You'll get a new job! Just wait and see!
Everyone does it!"*

"And prices for houses are going up," yelled the real
estate agent. *"If you don't buy now, you'll never have a
chance to own your own home—never, ever **again!**"*

Alice in Credit Land

So Alice gave them her savings to go find a mortgage.
All 50 pennies of it.

And the broker went off to Wall Street to find a mortgage
for Alice.

That night, Alice went to the Happy Hope Executive
Retraining School to find a job that pays more.

It was very inspiring. She heard about all sorts of careers
that paid lots of money:

FULFILL YOUR DREAMS! MAKE MORE $$$!"

"JD, MD, PhD, MBA, RA, MAI, CPA, CFA,
DDS! Online!"

The next day, the real estate agent and the mortgage broker returned with a mortgage from Wall Street.

"Well, you don't make enough money right now to qualify for the best mortgage. So we are going to have to charge you 25 pennies a month," said the broker.

"Instead of 20 pennies a month," said the real estate agent.

"For the first year," said the broker.

"But I can't afford 25 pennies a month. I don't have the better job yet. I still only make 40 pennies a month. I won't be able to eat or buy gas."

"My dear girl, that's what credit cards are for. And now that you have a mortgage, it's so easy to get one," said the real estate agent.

*"Or two or **three** or four!"* said the broker.

So, Alice went to the banks and got some credit cards.

The very next day, all of the food and gas prices went up.

It wasn't so very long after that when the King and
Queen decided that subjects throughout the kingdom had
far too much credit card debt.

So it was decreed that all credit card debt should be paid
back to the banks twice as fast.

So, the monthly payments on all of Alice's credit cards went from 5 pennies a month to 10 pennies a month.

All of a sudden, Alice discovered that she didn't have enough pennies in her paycheck to pay for the mortgage and all the credit cards.

She had to skip a payment or two—every month.

This made her credit card banks very unhappy.

"Not having enough money to pay our credit card bill is not an acceptable excuse!!!!!"

So, the credit card banks doubled the interest rates on Alice's cards and charged her huge delinquency fees.

This raised her credit card payments from 10 pennies a month to 20 pennies a month.

This made it even harder for Alice to pay her debts.

Then the King and Queen determined that subjects throughout the kingdom were still borrowing too much money. So they decided to raise interest rates to discourage people from borrowing more.

The interest rates on Alice's credit cards could not go up any higher because there's a law. That was the good news.

The bad news was that the interest rate on Alice's mortgage doubled. And so did her mortgage payment. It went to 50 pennies a month. From 25 pennies.

Then the house of cards blew down.

And the creek rose.

Alice in Credit Land

And the Happy Hope Executive Retraining School
disappeared and took away all of her hopes of getting a
new job.

Then Alice got a foreclosure notice. People said they were going to take her house away.

Alice went to the real estate agent and the mortgage broker for help.

"No Problem! We'll refinance!!! We'll double the mortgage to 20,000 pennies. We'll pay off all of your credit cards. Just give us 50 pennies right now!!!" said the broker.

"But all my pennies are gone," said Alice

"YOU DON'T HAVE ANY MORE PENNIES?!!"
gasped the real estate agent.

"My piggy bank is empty," said Alice.

"THEN YOU CAN'T KEEP YOUR HOUSE!"
screamed the real estate agent.

"But where will I live?" asked Alice.

"No problem! There aren't any pennies in the piggy
bank—***am I right?!"*** asked the real estate agent.

"Y-y-y-yes," admitted Alice.

***"THEN THERE'S PLENTY OF SPACE IN IT—FOR
YOU!"*** he screamed.

And with that, they took the deed to Alice's dream house
and stuffed her into the piggy bank.

Alice in Credit Land

Alice did not think this was fair.

From inside her piggy bank she yelled, **"I want my pennies back!!"**

"Ingrate," sputtered the real estate agent, as he fled to his next customer. "She's got a place to live—what's to complain about?"

"Go talk to Wall Street," suggested the mortgage broker helpfully, as he headed out over the hill.

So Alice went to Wall Street to ask for her pennies back.

"I want my pennies back," said Alice.

But Wall Street had nothing to say.

So Alice went to the government to complain.

"I want my pennies back."

"Get in line."

Alice got in line.

There were many people in line.

They were all waiting to see the King and Queen.

There was a lot of weeping and gnashing of teeth.

Great painful wailing came from way up at the front of
the line.

The wailing came from Slow Otto who couldn't sell cars, and Fast Banx who invested in bonds (or something like that).

They wanted some pennies too.

Trillions.

At last, Alice got an audience with the King.

"*WHO ARE YOU?*" asked the King.

"I'm Alice and I want my pennies back," said Alice.

"*How Many Pennies?*"
asked the King.

"Fifty."

"*What? What?? You Come Into Our Presence For Such A Pittance?!*"
roared the King.

"I'm hungry," mumbled Alice.

So the King ushered Alice over to see the Queen.

"She Says She's Hungry,"

said the King.

"I'm hungry," said Alice.

"Off With Her Head!"

said the Queen.

Alice in Credit Land

Suddenly a great quiet fell on the crowd.

Wall Street appeared in the sky.

There was much whispering.

Finally the King spoke:

"The Sentence of Death is Commuted. You Now Have Permission to Keep Your Head."

And then the Queen decreed:

"You Are Now Required to Buy Things!!"

Alice in Credit Land

But Alice didn't have any pennies to buy anything with.

So the Queen gave Alice a new credit card.

And Alice lived happily hand-to-mouth ever after.

www.ingramcontent.com/pod-product-compliance
Lightning Source LLC
Chambersburg PA
CBHW051235200326
41519CB00025B/7383